PREFACE

"The will to win isn't anywhere near so exceptionally significant as the will to get ready to win."
- Vince Lombardi

Preparation is the way to progress. "Karma" is the place where planning meets an amazing open door. Arrangement to convey implies rehearsing what you will impart. Similarly as one would get ready to "see about tying the knot", a business person should plan to speak with financial backers, fellow benefactors, workers, clients, accomplices, and vendors.

It is the sole liability of the pioneer, the business visionary, to convey the vision of the venture, for in the event that the individual can't impart the vision - the future - then how might anybody have confidence in that vision?

Excellent correspondence isn't arbitrary. It isn't fortunate. It is ready, rehearsed, culminated after some time, similar to a golf swing, mental durability, or even a satire act.

INTRODUCTION

"Great leaders must have two things: a vision of the world that does not yet exist and the ability to communicate that vision clearly." - Simon Sinek

Imagine what is happening: there are two business visionaries, each with precisely the same thought, ability, time, money, timing, and organization. Which business person succeeds and which one fails?

To respond to that inquiry, I'll pose another inquiry: how do business people gain footing for their thought? Straightforward response, they inform individuals. They could utilize the telephone, an advertisement, a blog, video, webcast, online entertainment, email, or in a real sense tell individuals in the city. Anything strategies they use to impart their message, they start with words.

The business visionary who conveys better will generally find success than one who can't convey well. Continuously. It was for this very explanation that I made Pitch Practice.

It is that "capacity to convey" that lies at the core of Pitch Practice. Over the beyond four and a half years, we have heard a great many pitches. That experience has prompted arranging Pitch Practice down to six basic places and 21 illustrations about those focuses. These focuses and examples are the meat of this book.

Chapter 1 - A Brief History of Pitch Practice

"You don't have to make your subject and verb agree to serve. You only need a heart full of grace. A soul generated by love." - Martin Luther King Jr.

In the late spring of 2013, I was dealing with my startup, Deductmor. Deductmor was a portable application for independently employed people to catch every one of their receipts with their telephone camera and supplement those costs into QB or anything bookkeeping bundle they utilized. I needed to raise some capital, however I had bootstrapped my initial 4 new businesses. Regardless of going through an IPO and two acquisitions, I had no clue about how to raise money.

While I was on a startup scholarship at Atlanta Tech Village and mentoring entrepreneurs at ATDC, I found out about "Pitch Gauntlet", a monthly meetup led by the principles at Venture Lab at Georgia Tech. I went to Pitch Gauntlet three months straight, and got pummeled with insight like clockwork, yet it wasn't sufficient practice for me to refine my pitch. I inquired as to whether they would consider doing the meetup on a more regular basis. They pleasantly declined, so I went to the people at ATV and inquired as to whether I could begin a week by week meetup gathering to assist me and different business visionaries with rehearsing our pitches.

On June 27th, 2013, the meetup now referred to as Pitch Practice was brought into the world as "Startup BP", which was a baseball similarity for "taking batting practice." Three weeks from that point forward, we changed the name to Pitch Practice. After two years, the Village named a meeting room "The Pitch Practice Boardroom."

LESSON 1: Solve an issue, regardless of whether it's only for you toward the start. No one can tell who it will help.

Chapter 2 - How Pitch Practice Works

"It's the little details that are vital. Little things make big things happen." - John Wooden

The picture underneath gives a brief look at how we structure the work of art "short presentation". This design isn't the good news of pitch. You're not going to damnation on the off chance that you don't follow it, however it works.

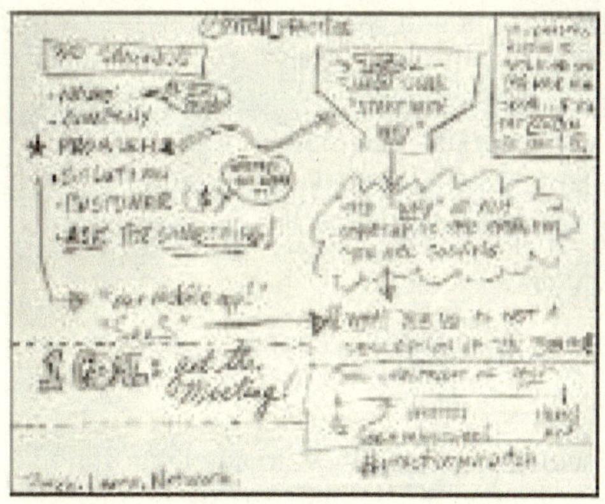

We start with the 30-second pitch, focusing on the problem, as explained in Simon Sinek's TED Talk "Start with Why." Then we build out to the 3-minute "contest" pitch and then the 5-6 minute investor pitch.

Why do we do it thusly? Since it's a lot more straightforward to begin with nothing, assemble something little, then, at that point, add to it than it is to begin with 20 minutes of death-by-powerpoint and inquire, "what can we cut?"

Cut everything and begin with the issue you're solving.

"80% of success is just showing up." - Woody Allen

You simply never know. At the point when I began Pitch Practice, I couldn't say whether anyone
would come to a meetup to test out your plan to outsiders. I still actually never know who will make an appearance, who will pitch, for sure they are going to pitch.

Every Friday, I set up in the Pitch Practice Boardroom at ATV, have some Startup Chowdown lunch, and see who makes an appearance. Now and again there are 7, and once in a while there are 100.

Is it still a "meetup" assuming there are just 2 attendees?

Yes, it is. Quite some time ago, when my significant other and I began a local area Bible review at our home, we had a ton of to and fro about who'll be there that evening and who will not and we now and then wavered on "would it be advisable for us we drop tonight?"

Then we settled on the choice that, regardless of the number of individuals appeared or didn't appear, we were having Bible review on Tuesday evenings at 630PM, period. No more inquiries, no more IFs. You appear, you get taken care of (truly and spiritually).

Same goes for Pitch Practice. Assuming one individual appears, we'll increase the value of their pitch, period.

That has occurred over and over. Once, an understudy from a neighborhood programming dev school at ATV appeared, and we talked for 30 minutes about a thought the understudy has. He messed up the same way that many individuals have made before him: he had a thought looking for an issue to solve.

He truly battled to express the issue that he could settle, yet we in the end arrived. He was stirred up about this thought when he showed up, and he left significantly more invigorated in light of the fact that he had some build, some setting around which to form his task. All the more significantly, he comprehended how to impart to others about his thought and the issue that it solves.

LESSON 2: be reliable. Appear arranged without fail. Since you simply never know.

Chapter 3 - Pitch Practice is a Service

"A lot of times, people don't know what they want until you show it to them." - Steve Jobs

I began Pitch Practice to help me, and it has turned into a local area vehicle for helping other people. That is the "why" of Pitch Practice: *new business people don't have any idea how to convey their worth.* At the point when you work from "why" and take care of a genuine issue, you find incalculable advantages as you do as such. I would never have anticipated that as a result from 4 ½ years (and then some) of Pitch Practice.

Question: Work on Weaknesses or Play to Strengths?·Reply: Yes.

Do a SWOT (Strengths, Shortcomings, Potential open doors, Threats) investigation on you. Whether you're in a task with a steady organization, a full-time business visionary, or considering a startup, you need to know your assets, weaknesses, opportunities, and dangers. In particular, in the event that you're beginning a business, you would do well to know your assets and shortcomings, and afterward practice what you specialize in and defeat what you do worst.

There are multiple ways of doing both. Here is my rundown of my thought process are a portion of my assets and shortcomings. I did this practice in 2014, it actually remains constant today.

Strengths

1. No fear of failure. I've failed before. It sucks, but life goes on. You figure out how to get to tomorrow, pay the bills, fill that hole, plug that leak, etc. Do I think about failing? Sure, who doesn't? But to me, it's like dying. I don't fear death. I fear dying. Big difference.
2. Leading little groups. I just did sort of a stock of my week by week timetable, and I understand that I lead, or have an influential position in, seven little teams.
3. Quick review. There's very little I can't learn, assuming I need to and on the off chance that I

   set my focus on it. I learned item the board in 1996 when I had never seen it done. I learned WiFi. I learned WordPress. I learned barely sufficient HTML to be risky. I've picked up publicly supporting, AWS, Google Apps, and Mechanical Turk. I love to learn and am not scared of picking up something new.

4. I get innovation. I can't compose code or plan an organization, however I get it, and I can identify BS from the best Systems Engineer and make sense of why it's BS to the deals and showcasing team.

Weaknesses

1. *Procrastination - assuming there's no due date, I will keep away from it at all costs until there is a date, then I'll do it.*
2. *I can't compose code - I can make a HTML table, yet not much more.*
3. *I can't sell - It's the course of deals that I suck at.*
4. *I'm awful at systems administration - Introverts join together! Organizing occasions exhaust me.*
5. *I will more often than not get occupied by the little things.*

Naturally, I attempt overall quite well to take advantage of my natural abilities, and do things I've done well previously and realize I can do once more. With respect to my shortcomings, those drive two or three things I do consistently, in light of the fact that you can conceal your shortcomings for such a long time. In the long run, in the tension of a startup, your assets will sparkle and your shortcomings (and those of your group) will be uncovered. It's the means by which you beat these shortcomings that counts.

To conquer my hesitation, I make a rundown of all that I should finish consistently. The rundown lives until it's completely done, regardless of whether that is in seven days' time. I recruit sales reps and programming designers on the grounds that regardless of whether I advanced either or both, I won't ever be basically as great as an expert at all things considered. To defeat my poor systems administration capacities I complete a few things, deliberately and purposefully:

1. I run Pitch Practice consistently. This meetup has turned into a customary piece of my week after week cadence, and I've met many business visionaries, financial backers, and just for the most part overall quite accommodating people.
2. I served from the barrel at "Atlanta Startup Village" for a long time. I

met each individual who got through the entryway for a lager. I had to.

It's not my normal adapted to meet individuals suddenly. I'm not the person who has "never met a more peculiar." I can't "work a room." I've watched others do it flawlessly, yet that is not me. To beat that shortcoming, I put myself in cars moving the opposite direction, as it were, and deliberately meet everybody I can in that surge of people.

Pitch Practice offers me the chance to meet, help, and gain from different business people as they work on making sense of their business. Filling cups with lager at Startup Village managed the cost of me the delight of saying "Hey! How're you!" to 400 individuals each month.

LESSON 3: to beat your shortcomings, figure out how to serve others as you incorporate those shortcomings into qualities. That is all Pitch Practice at any point was or alternately is: a way for me to serve different business visionaries by utilizing my assets and experience. You have qualities and experience, too.

LESSON 4: Having a develop in which to make your pitch is critical. Very much like when you start a business, you want a few limits, a plan of action, something whereupon to base how you approach everything on an everyday premise, you want a spot to begin and a few limits around your pitch.

Chapter 4 - Practice Makes Perfect

"Pitching is an acquired skill, not an innate talent, Kawasaki says. It takes practice." - Guy Kawasaki

I had an extraordinary chance to talk about Pitch Practice and about contributing general to an extremely different crowd at ROAM Dunwoody. The crowd wasn't simply tech new companies. That made me ponder "the pitch" as a general rule, and not similarly as I see it through my tech startup lens.

Everybody - everyone - is pitching constantly. No one at any point mulls over everything, substantially less practices it. But you should. Everybody ought to rehearse their pitch. Rehearsing is essential for being ready, such as charging your telephone, conveying a pen or your business card. The following are five reasons you should rehearse your pitch.

1. You never realize who you're going to meet.
2. You would rather not sound canned, mechanical, or rehearsed.
3. Preparation is the most ideal way to answer opportunity.
4. Everyone adores a decent speaker and presentation.
5. You may just get one shot.

At the occasion at ROAM, I made a solid point that Pitch Practice was made considering tech new businesses, however that the standards of conveying an incredible short presentation, 3-minute pitch, or 5-minute financial backer deck are something very similar, regardless of what your identity is for sure you're pitching. Your story should propel. Your conveyance should be regular. Your source of inspiration should be clear.

Delivering an incredible pitch or show, similar to whatever else throughout everyday life, requires practice. Before a mirror, before your canine, video recorded on your telephone, or with an accommodating gathering like Pitch Practice. Regardless of how you get ready, you should prepare.

Always Be Pitching

Now that you realize that you forever are pitching, you can deliberately forever be pitching. On the whole, a haiku about being prepared:

Frequent explorers
have a mantra - A.B.C.
Continuously be
charging

At a new tech local area occasion, I was helped to remember something that we as a whole realize we ought to be continuously doing, back in the openings of our psyches, however don't regularly contemplate. But we should be thinking about it because to be good at anything means being intentional about it. At that occasion, obviously one of the moderators had invested some genuine energy, also movement, into their pitch. They were deliberate about their message, their energy, and their planning (5:00 on the dot).

This point of view is an immense piece of Pitch Practice. There were presumably around 300+ individuals at that occasion. Consider the last systems administration occasion you joined in. What number of individuals asked you, “Anyway, what do you do?” what number individuals did you pose that equivalent inquiry? Assuming you’re organizing, and you need to be critical to individuals you meet (in an expert way), then you ought to remember that you are continuously pitching. You’re continuously pitching yourself. Whenever you let somebody know what you do, for sure you’ve done, for sure you’re intending to do, you are pitching, since no one can tell who your next boss, client, accomplice, worker, or financial backer is going to be.

And, a haiku to finish this thought.

All entrepreneurs
Always pitching, constantly
You simply never know

Always be pitching. Intentionally.

How long should my elevator pitch be?

An incessant subject of conversation at Pitch Practice is the ideal opportunity for the brief presentation. Why 30 seconds? Whenever you’re really in a lift, time the ride. It’s normally considerably less than 30 seconds. So for what reason do we base an elevator pitch on that unit of time?

The basic response is this: you have to begin some place. You truly don’t require 30 seconds to make yourself clear. We utilize 30 seconds as an inconsistent apparatus for incorporating discipline into your words about what it is that you do. But why?

Another basic solution to that inquiry is that, when somebody asks you what you do for sure your startup is about, the last thing you need to do is make them look at their watch after you’ve been babbling on for 3 or 4 minutes. Try not to do that.

Limiting your short presentation to 30 seconds is tied in with making yourself clear concisely and really. Those two simply end up matching with bring brief. The justification for curtness ought to be self-evident, however to an extraordinary number of individuals, it’s not. Whenever you initially meet somebody or somebody poses you a sharp inquiry (e.g., "what's your startup do?"), it's simply affable to cut to the chase, particularly where this sort of inquiry most frequently occurs: at systems administration meetings.

Just like we put lines on a field or court, edges on a record, limits on the characters in a tweet, and size improvements on a picture for a social post, it's about discipline. Thirty seconds is totally erratic, yet the activity of making an example of words that stands out of your audience and forces some activity in less than 30 seconds is the same than the demonstration of chipping golf balls into a 5-gallon can from shifting distances.

Practicing your contribute is tied in with learning discipline your words.

Time Goes By Quickly

Time elapses so rapidly, both in the full scale and micro.

In the macro, guess what? It's already________________. How'd that happen? We get busy. We plan each week in minute detail, and plan each weekend with wild abandon so we make sure we don't get to bed on Sunday night and wonder what we did with our weekend. There's basketball season (March Madness! Go Duke!), football season (Go Dawgs!), high school & middle

school soccer season, and spring break. What's more, in no time, you'll make Memorial Day weekend plans.

In the miniature, my Digital Marketing class experienced how quick five minutes passes in cruel reality on "Demo Night", when every understudy allowed a 5 moment (no more!) show of their undertaking. Whenever I contributed with "one moment!", no less than 8 of the understudies took a gander at me with sickening dread and said "Wha… ? Truly??" Five minutes is a truly lengthy pitch, yet for these new advertisers, it was like snapping your fingers.

I asked a short time later the number of understudies had polished their introductions ahead of time: *six out of 17 understudies had really said the words and strolled through their slides before Demo Night*. Those six people had encountered how quick time elapses when you're up before 50 individuals introducing the work that you have created.

Others were exceptionally ready. On somewhere around 3 events, when I said "one moment", the moderators took a gander at me and unobtrusively said, “Alright,” and tapped on their “Thank you/Q&A” slide. Boom.

Whatever you’re doing, assuming you will be planned, you would do well to rehearse before the genuine deal.

You’ll never say it like that in real life!

One of the greatest “complaints” (put in statements since it ordinarily appears to be a disapprove of offensive remark) to “rehearsing your pitch” that I’ve heard is this:

“You’re never going to say that in real life!”

We work on saying the short presentation again and again and over, endlessly, until we get it “right.” But it’s valid. You never will say it precisely as you do at Pitch Practice. Here are some other things you will never, ever do.

- You won’t ever shuffle a soccer ball on your feet, thighs, shoulders, and head multiple times during a genuine soccer game.
- You won’t ever hit a 7-iron 50 straight times from the equivalent spot

focusing on a similar objective in a genuine golf tournament.

- You won’t ever take 25 three-pointers from a similar spot on the floor with no protection in a genuine b-ball game.
- You won’t ever hit a handling faker in a genuine football game.
- You won’t ever hit 100 straight serves in a genuine tennis match.
- You won’t ever shuffle a baseball on the bat in a genuine game.
- You won’t ever turn a b-ball on your finger in a genuine game.
- You won’t ever convey a 5-minute financial backer deck without interferences, questions, or remarks from genuine investors.

The more you follow through with Along these linesmething - anything - the better you get at doing that thing. So, no, you won’t ever warmly greet a total more unusual and afterward continue through a canned, practiced brief presentation. You will, notwithstanding, offer a response to “anyway, what do you do?” or “what’s your startup do?”

Are you prepared to offer that response? Have you worked on saying the words before genuine individuals who are not hesitant to make you feel awful and give you genuine, objective criticism? That is our specialty at Pitch Practice consistently, and that is the place where you can rehearse the words you will convey when somebody asks you, "Thus, what do you do?"

So, next time you're swinging away with that 7-iron, consider how much certainty that training gives you on the course and apply that equivalent system to how you articulate what you do.

LESSON 3: Practice makes awesome. Become so familiar with your pitch that you don't sound canned. That requires some investment. Until you say it without holding back, before genuine individuals, no one can tell how it's going to sound.

LESSON 4: Until you stand up and do it before genuine individuals, you don't realize that your hands never emerged from your pockets or that you influence to and fro or never take a gander at anyone.

Chapter 5 - The Pitch Practice Methodology

"People don't buy what you do, they buy why you do it." - Simon Sinek

When I began Pitch Practice in June of 2013, I didn't have any idea what it would ultimately be for sure worth it could need to other people. It was basically a tomfoolery social affair of individual business people to help each other response the inquiry, "In this way, *what do you do?" somewhat better*, and furthermore assist us with getting ready for occasions like Atlanta Startup Village or Startup Riot or any of the many pitch challenges that appear to continue to spring up. The week after week occasion positively has achieved every one of those goals.

However, it was only after running the gathering for an over eighteen months that I observed two TED talks that totally had an impact on the manner in which I lead Pitch Practice, and the manner in which I help startup business people (a) foster their short presentation and (b) recount their story.

- Simon Sinek, “How Great Leaders Inspire Action”
- Nancy Duarte, “The mystery design of incredible talks”

In fostering a 30-second brief presentation, I fostered the pitch practice structure, and have involved it in each pitch talk since.

A somewhat more profound explanation:

1. Your Name
2. Your Organization (assuming you have one yet)
3. **The Problem you’re solving**
4. Your Solution to that problem
5. Customer (who will pay you money?)
6. Ask - what do you need?

There’s no set in stone request, and you don’t need to utilize this large number of components in the event that you would rather not, however this is a spot to begin, a construction, a bunch of boundaries

that will assist you with getting from a clear piece of paper to an extremely short and expressive short presentation that you can tell anybody and they’ll get it.

Focus on the Problem

“Issue” is in intense above in light of the fact that that is the place where your center ought to be assuming you’re beginning a tech business today. We get this construction from the Lean Startup Methodology, arranged by Eric Ries and Steve Blank. The essential principle is that you don’t think of good thoughts. Rather, you make answers for huge costly issues. In this way, on the off chance that you’re not tackling an agonizing business sector issue, you could need to reconsider your idea.

Your concentration in your 30-second pitch ought to be almost all the way on articulating the issue. While you’re conversing with your appropriate interest group, they will all “get it” since they are living with that issue today (that is the way you realize they are your legitimate interest group), and they will promptly need to find out about your solution.

That gets us to the principal TED talk that motivates Pitch Practice (sorry it took such a long time), in which Simon Sinek splendidly makes sense of that individuals don’t buy your “what” they purchase your “why”. Sinek alludes to Apple as one of the instances of how a brand can be so great at their "why" that it doesn't make any difference what their "what" really is. How could you purchase a music player or a telephone or a watch from a PC company?

Because you realize it will break every one of the recently characterized limits, very much like the Macintosh did in 1984, the iPod did in 2001, the iPhone in 2007, the iPad in 2010, and perhaps the iWatch in 2015, or the Apple HomePod in 2018.

Start With Why

In your pitch, the issue you are addressing is your "why", and is the focal point of all your energy and words. Whenever you can work on an enormous market issue into only a couple of words so your kid or your 85-year-old grandma comprehends it, then you really get it and can pass your vision for tackling that issue on to anyone.

Too frequently, good thoughts are introduced by business people who have no desire,
readiness, or construction for recounting to their story, so the issue goes inexplicable until a "visionary" who can zero in on the "why" enters the market.

"If you can't explain it simply, you don't understand it well enough." - Albert Einstein

The subsequent TED talk includes truly recounting to your story in a pitch significantly longer than 30 seconds, and is a touch more intricate, however staggeringly strong when used appropriately. A piece of Apple's astounding achievement is the capacity of its originator, Steve Jobs, to keep his crowd anxious. Nancy Duarte investigates the discourse Jobs gave in presenting the iPhone in 2007 and Martin Luther King, Jr's."I have a fantasy" discourse. She took apart the two talks so completely as to draw out a deliberate and strong example that keeps the crowd completely connected with and on the edge of their seats.

The actual example is basic: down and all over and all over. However, what's the significance here to the business person pitching their startup to a group of people? It truly is basic, but then so powerful.

This straightforward example of conveying the crowd to new highs and new lows consistently incredibly affects the audience members, basically by keeping them completely connected with until the pinnacle of the discourse wherein the arrangement is shared and the vision cast.

I had paid attention to and given ideas for many tests out from a wide range of business sectors and business visionaries, however until I heard and applied Sinek and Duarte's TED Talks to Pitch Practice, everything depended on nothing other than, "that appears to work better".

Having a design to anything fixes things such that a lot less difficult to start, and having a construction to your pitch and your story can convey your startup far towards success.

Pitch Practice is a Starting Point

Over the long stretches of Pitch Practice, we've heard the accompanying expression a considerable amount: "I'm not quite certain where to begin." It's normal, and it's alright. One of the best

devices to emerge from these beyond 3 years that truly helps new business visionaries is the build that we give from which anybody can make an extraordinary pitch.

Having a develop in which to make your pitch is essential. Very much like when you start a business, you really want a few limits, a plan of action, something whereupon to base how you approach everything on an everyday premise, you want a spot to begin and a few limits around your pitch.

Given a green field and an open mic, a great many people tend towards sending off into an extended clarification of what they do. While that can be great on occasion, it generally leaves the crowd inquiring, "Uh, so what's that have to do with me?" Your pitch isn't about you. Your pitch is about the gathering for whom you offer a support, in particular the assistance of taking care of some issue or other. Your interest group - not you - ought to be the star of the show.

That's the place where the build that has come from 2,000+ pitches centers: the issue. Motivated by Sinek's TED Talk, book, and resulting development, the "why" of a startup is the issue that the startup is solving.

It's straightforward. I've broken down the line, "It's not the gospel. *You're not going to Hell on the off chance that you don't utilize it, however it works.*" So, I'll stay with it. Pitch Practice is a beginning stage. The absolute best pitches we've heard scarcely contact this build, and it surely doesn't need to be in a specific order.

It turns out best for yourself as well as your crowd. What you say best, what rolls off the tongue the best, and what makes yourself clear to your crowd most really. The six marks of the Pitch Practice strategy are a beginning stage, nothing more.

Boil it down

OK, so you have this thought, and you've conversed with a lot of people in-regulation about it, and it's beginning to sound good… to you. Remember, you were wrong the first time, right? Then you were wrong again the second and third times, right? It's ok. Anybody who has at any point begun a business and owned it as far as possible (great, awful, or revolting) misunderstands been no less than once, and those cases of being totally off-base merit a few slides in

their talking commitment. However, presently you have your arms around this thing, right?

Now reduce it down. Work on it. Let's assume it so your kid or your grandma gets it and can without much of a stretch tell anybody they know about your psycho thought. Can't make it happen? Then you don't get it yet yourself.

Here's a basic activity that we train at Pitch Practice to assist the holders of groundbreaking thoughts with reducing them down. Ask yourself the accompanying questions:

1. What's the issue you're solving?
2. What's your answer for the problem?
3. Who will pay for your solution?

Let's utilization super hot Atlanta startup Calendly as an example.

- What's the issue? Messaging to and fro and to and fro attempting to set aside a decent opportunity to meet with somebody is tedious and drawn-out. We've all done this before.
- What's Calendly's answer for the issue? "Calendly assists you

with booking gatherings without the ever changing messages." Notice there's nothing about how they do it?

- Who will pay for it? Individuals and groups who plan arrangements or orchestrate meetings.

Did I find those solutions right? Would you be able to rehash that in 30 seconds? Provided that this is true, then, at that point, you comprehend, and can rehash and pitch Calendly's business. Presently, shouldn't something be said about yours?

Boil it down. The reduced clarification turns into the skeleton of your brief presentation. Remember it so it rolls off your tongue like the Pledge of Allegiance.

The First Step Towards Creating A Great Pitch

In 2015 and 2016, I showed 60+ classes and studios for General Assembly about web-based entertainment, Google Analytics, WordPress writing for a blog, advanced showcasing, advertising innovation, and different themes. At the beginning of a large portion of these meetings, everybody inquired, "Do I really want my computer?"

There are 2 reasons that participants pose this inquiry. In the first place, will they need their PC to really finish a particular responsibilities? Second, will they need their PC to take notes? The first is simple. The subsequent inquiry is an individual inclination, yet that inclination accompanies some science. Assuming you take notes by composing, you're putting yourself in a difficult situation, since when you record something, you recollect it better.

A similar kind of science applies to when you are making a new thing. Recording your objectives makes them "genuine". Composing somebody an individual "Card to say thanks" truly ups your relationship game. Recording your errands empowers you to confirm them individually, bringing a Dave Ramsey feeling of achievement. Likewise, when you see a word recorded, that sight brings out groundbreaking insights about that word, its significance to you, and its context.
Finally, when you record something, the actual demonstration of recording it seals it in your memory 7X better than seeing it, hearing it, or composing it.

As you've presumably speculated at this point, the initial move towards making an extraordinary pitch for your business or startup is to record it. In particular, record the accompanying points:

1. What is the issue your association is solving?
2. What is your answer for this problem?
3. Who is your most ideal customer?
4. What do you want today to prevail with regards to addressing the problem?

It's fundamentally significant for you, the organizer and pioneer, to know and see every one of these focuses each in its most personal detail. By what other means will you give this information to worker number 1 or representative 100? It's your light to convey, and you are the person who will impart these solutions to anybody and everyone.

An extra advance that I see as exceptionally accommodating for this exercise is to address each inquiry as, or if nothing else in the length of, a tweet: 140 characters in particular (#oldschool). Einstein said, "On the off chance that you can't make sense of it essentially, you don't comprehend it alright." I concur earnestly! You ought to have the option to make sense of how you treat a 5-year-old and your grandma simultaneously, and have the two of them by and large "get it."

Doing so requires curtness and straightforwardness. It's difficult, yet that is the reason we endlessly practice starts with whenever you first compose it down.

LESSON 5: You truly don't require 30 seconds to make yourself clear. We utilize 30 seconds as an erratic apparatus for incorporating discipline into your words about what it is that you do. Set your own bar for excellence, then practice and beat it.

Chapter 6 - Who Are You? You are the Jockey.

"Properly understood, any new and better way of doing things is technology." - Peter Thiel

If you request 10 from the main 10 funding firms or 10 of the best 10 tech startup gas pedals in the US what their #1 rule is for putting resources into or wagering on a startup, you'd find a really predictable solution: *"We bet on the rider, not the pony." Group*, team, team.

It's about the establishing group. With that information, including some chunk of data about you or your group in your pitch's basic. Obviously, everybody's experience is unique, so there's more than one approach to infusing your group's insight into a lift pitch.

Here are a few thoughts that line up with the Pitch Practice technique of developing your brief presentation, in view of the foundation of Shane Ballman, the originator and CEO of SynapseMX, a 500Startups graduate and early Pitch Practice attendee.

- Name - when you present yourself, it's not difficult to incorporate a brief tale, for example, "During my 15 years of overseeing plane upkeep at Southwest Airlines… "
- Problem - present your experience by making sense of how you found, approved, or tackled the issue you are tending to: "In the wake of persevering through this issue for a considerable length of time in the aircraft support space, I started assembling a group to make an answer for the problem."
- Solution - how could you concoct your answer? More often than not, the arrangement is conceived out of encountering the issue. "Our group has an aggregate of 85 years of involvement with the carrier upkeep space, and we've addressed the problem."
- Customer - If you've experienced the issue, approved the issue, and tackled the issue, you definitely know precisely who your objective client is, in light of your experience: "We've all worked in the aircraft business for 10+ years each, so we have critical relationship value with our client base."
- Ask - Sometimes, your experience can be your solidarity, yet it can likewise assist you with recognizing a need in your group. "Our establishing group is comprised of carrier upkeep engineers with many long stretches of involvement. We're effectively searching out big business deals experts with 5+ long periods of involvement with complex deals to the aircraft industry."

There are bunches of approaches to sharing your group's insight, and no two will at any point be something very similar; notwithstanding, your group's experience is straightforwardly connected with the odds of coming out on top for your startup. Experienced financial backers will base their assessment of your startup, essentially to some extent, on the experience of your team.

If you and your group have no insight, that doesn't preclude you from progress by any stretch of the imagination, however you really should claim it front and center. VC and gas pedals can smell BS a pretty far, and assuming you're 22 or 23 years of age, experience may not be your best resource. Own that front and center and move it by zeroing in on your ability, energy, and your capacity to gain from your advisors.

Trying out various ways of conveying your pitch is the explanation Pitch Practice exists in any case. As the people at FirstRound as of late said, "Practice is basic, *and the piece of the cycle is the most barely noticeable, procrastinated and underutilized.*" Every time you practice your pitch, you discover some new information, and each new pitch you hear, you gain some new useful knowledge that you can apply (or keep away from!) in your own pitch.

Someone has already stolen your idea

It hasn't occurred in a really long time, yet at the Pitch Practice meetup, it used to be a genuinely normal event. Somebody would join in, however say nothing until the last call of "Alright, who else might want to rehearse their pitch?" They'd constantly make some noise with something like the following:

> *"I truly need to do my pitch, yet we haven't marked any kind of NDA and you (addressing me, the meetup pioneer) haven't uttered a word about secrecy or non-competition."*

That's the point at which it would get sort of abnormal until I figured out how to deal with this definite circumstance. It's easy, meaning the words I use are basic and clear; be that as it may, the individual who raised this issue with sharing their pitch has earnest anxieties about sharing their thought. That should be viewed in a serious way in light of the fact that more often than not they have an experiential justification for not sharing more openly.

They've most likely been scorched previously. I think we as a whole skill that feels. I realize I do. You share something that you're truly amped up for with somebody you trust, and afterward half a month, months, or years after the fact, you discover that individual you trusted has taken your thought and gone for it. They took your idea.

That's a genuine article. No surprises there. Constantly. Thus, we should be conscious of that individual's insight and apprehension about being singed again.

But that doesn't change the reality of the situation, and that reality is: Anyone can take - and probably as of now has taken your thought. However, it's not possible for anyone to take your execution.

When you have a thought, you and you alone convey the vision for that thought and how it will look and figure out itself over the course of the following 1, 2, 5, 10 years. That is YOUR vision, and no other individual can see it or execute on it. That is your benefit. At times, that may be your main benefit. Accordingly, share your idea.

Someone has (without a doubt) currently taken it! They simply call it something other than what's expected and you have barely any familiarity with it yet. That is the thing we call "rivalry", and contest is great. Contest makes us work harder to be smarter to separate ourselves and push toward that vision.

Pitch Practice is tied in with rehearsing so you can improve. In the event that you can't expressive what you're doing, it will be truly challenging to get fellow benefactors, accomplices, financial backers, or clients. Assuming that you want to get a NDA from everyone

you converse with, how might you at any point get any criticism on if your thought is great or bad?

LESSON 6: If you have profound space aptitude, say it! That implies you've experienced this issue, and you comprehend who it influences the aftereffects of fixing that issue. It implies you have credibility.

LESALONG THESE LINESN 7: Anyone can take your thought. It's not possible for anyone to take your execution. So, share your thought. Somebody as of now has taken it! They simply call it something other than what's expected and you have close to zero insight into it yet. Assuming you need to get a NDA from everybody you converse with, you're ill-fated from the start.

Chapter 7 - The Problem

"Success is not delivering a feature; success is learning how to solve the customer's problem." - Eric Ries

In both Pitch Practice and in my work with my substance advertising clients, perhaps the most difficult undertaking is making sure about the issue explanation. Pretty much every time I pose the inquiry at Pitch Practice, "what is the issue that [insert startup name here] is tackling?" the response I get is a decent depiction of what the startup does.

> ***What your startup does is not the same thing as the problem your startup is attempting to solve.***

Again, we return to three assets that have enormously helped me in driving Pitch Practice as well as coaching startup business visionaries and pitching my own ventures:

- The Lean Startup – We don't start businesses with great ideas. We start organizations to settle a major, frightful, bristly, smelling issue in an industry we know.
- Start with Why – Your "why" is the problem you're solving… the problem that you know about, have lived with, understand, and can solve.
- The secret structure of great talks – Telling a great story is a science, and there is a story behind how you arrived at your solution to this great big problem.

These equivalent things once more?!? Indeed. An exceptionally astute tutor of mine says regularly, "Great correspondence is predictable and dreary. Great correspondence is steady and monotonous." We have Pitch Practice week by week for this very reason.

Now, from every one of these awesome assets and the blend of the three, the business visionary can now (a) concoct an incredible business thought, (b) comprehend how to make an advertising message as well as art a strong pitch, and (c) figure out how to create an extraordinary story around the business.

With those bolts in your quiver, how about we take on the issue articulation. The following are five qualities of the issue statement:

1. It's not about you, Mr. Serial Entrepreneur with a wide range of incredible ideas.
2. It's about your objective client, their aggravation or their concern or their impediment throughout everyday life or in business.
3. It's a depiction of something broken, wasteful, old or obsolete.
4. It's your justification for existing as a startup (you're not kidding "business" yet)
5. It's something you've lived in or around for a huge timeframe (space expertise)

With the comprehension of these 5 attributes of the issue, you currently include a few limits inside which to attempt to make an extraordinary issue proclamation that will right away catch your crowd's eye. Your explanation of the issue will strike a chord with your crowd (the right crowd) since they, as well, have lived with the aggravation of this issue for years.

Use this build when you set off to foster your concern articulation. That is the place where everything begins. Assuming everything looks great explanation, there's no business.

Focus on the Problem

Since we currently concur that great correspondence is predictable and redundant, continuing to show exactly the same things again and again's alright. Consistently at Pitch Practice we pay attention to twelve or so pitches from new business visionaries about novel thoughts. We start with (a token of) the basic strategy for creating your
30-second pitch:

- Your name
- Your organization name (assuming that you have one yet)
- What's the issue you are solving
- What's your solution
- Who is your client (who pays you money?)
- What do you want (otherwise known as the ask)?

This Pitch Practice structure is an erratic technique. There's no science behind it, other than it fills in as a fundamental construction for figuring out how to try out your thought, your organization, your item, or even you assuming you're looking for business or provisional labor. You don't need to work in the above request, and at times it's more compelling to say your name last so that part will be all the more effectively remembered.

In utilizing this design, two things perpetually happen:

1. People get the arrangement mistaken for the problem
2. People experience issues sorting out some way to express the issue momentarily, actually, and in a way that makes the crowd "get it" immediately.

The primary issue is truly one of semantics. I inquire, "What's the issue XYZ startup is settling?", and somebody generally answers with a great portrayal of what XYZ startup does, however not what the issue is. The two are totally different. Check whether you can depict the issue, as opposed to what the organization does (or means to do), in light of the fact that everything thing any new startup can manage is tackle a major problem.

My idea to any individual who staggers here is this: emphasis on the issue. Chris Turner of Ten Rocket nailed this from the beginning with a genuine issue, particularly in Atlanta. His pitch resembled this:

"Entrepreneurs have great ideas, but those ideas rarely make it to the MVP."

He's changed it since he began Ten Rocket, primarily on the grounds that his MVP-building startup has had such a lot of achievement, yet the center continues as before. He zeroed in on the issue, and in doing so left the arrangement in the eyes and ears of the crowd. Everybody in the Atlanta tech startup community

knows and can ordinarily connect with the issue of having an extraordinary thought yet not being a product designer and not having the option to view an accessible programming engineer as a fellow benefactor. It's a gigantic problem!

It's not you. It's me.

I once drove a the entire day course at General Assembly in Atlanta. This class was a 6-hour occasion in which we packed the 60 hours of the General Assembly Digital Marketing class down to 6 hours, with lunch from Chipotle included.

The occasion had a few difficulties: the Ponce City Market power went out on Friday night, leaving us with no cooling the entire day Saturday. In July. In Atlanta. You heard that right. It arrived at 80 degrees in our homeroom, yet the many swaying fans and frozen yogurt sandwiches and popsicles caused us to feel cherished anyway.

So, we utilized this real, actual issue to talk about the principal part of computerized showcasing: marking. One of the most apparent parts of your image is your message. What you say matters. Each word matters, on the grounds that your image is all that you do. We utilized a straightforward activity to exhibit the point that each word matters. Here is that straightforward exercise.

Answer every one of these 4 inquiries as a tweet, utilizing 140 characters (#oldschool) or less. Add a picture assuming you like, assuming that that represents your image, yet the 140 characters ought to likewise stand alone.

1. *What are your center values?*
2. *What industry or market issue are you solving?*
3. *Who is your ideal client and how would you reach them?*
4. *Describe your business.*

It's a decent method for finding out (a) in the event that you know your image and (b) how well you know your image. We walk through this exercise because if you, as the founder or entrepreneur or brand ambassador don't know your brand, how can you communicate that brand to anyone else, inside or outside the company?

We start with the second piece of this activity: "what is the business or market issue you are settling?" In making this little activity, the motivation for this progression is - sit tight for it! - Simon Sinek's 2009 TED Talk and book, "Begin with Why."

The class did this activity, requiring around 15 minutes to make the 4 tweets. Where we ran into the most over the top difficulty was this progression number 2. It is a pattern: *business people have incredible trouble recognizing the issue proclamation from the portrayal of their business*. At the end of the day, when I inquire "what issue are you addressing?" the response I get most frequently is “we do various things, *making esteem to a great extent and saving our clients time and cash with these advantages*,” and afterward they continue to list all the benefits.

This answer is completely wrong, and it starts with the first word, “we”.

The issue you are tackling has literally nothing to do with “we” or “us” or “I” or “me”. The issue you are tackling is an issue out in the market that your client has. Whenever you are conversing with a possible client and that client hears (endlessly) what you do, you’ve lost them. Whenever you start with the issue that your client has consistently (begin with why), you make a companion. They presently realize that you see and comprehend their problem.
And, in particular, that you tackle that problem.

“It’s not you. It’s me.” - Seinfeld, The Lip Reader, Season 5, Episode 6

When you’re stating your problem, remember “it’s not you, it’s me”, and “me” is your customer. Everything unquestionably revolves around the client’s concern. Your concern explanation doesn’t have anything to do with you. Rather, it’s the reason you exist. Begin with why. Begin with the issue, and settle it.

Defining the problem is very hard

Every week at Pitch Practice, we go through a basic activity with each pitch. After the business visionary conveys their pitch, I pose the gathering the accompanying inquiries, to perceive how well the message of the pitch was gotten. As may be obvious, these inquiries just certify the six marks of the Pitch
Practice structure.

1. What is his/her name?
2. What is the association name?
3. What is the issue they are attempting to solve?
4. Who is the customer?
5. What is their solution?
6. What did they ask for?

Generally, these are quite simple inquiries to respond to; be that as it may, the reason behind posing these inquiries of the crowd (the pitching business visionary isn't permitted to answer except if we stall out) is to decide whether, and how well, the speaker's message got past. More often than not, we stall out on a few of these focuses for different reasons. But one question gets people tripped up every single week: *what is the problem they are trying to solve?*

Without fall flat, when we pose this inquiry, somebody will respond to it with an exact depiction of what the startup does, and they are totally off-base. What the startup or business does isn't a depiction of the issue. My go-to line here is this:

> ***"if you use the words I, me, my, we, our, or us in your description of the problem, you are wrong."***

The issue you are tackling - your "why" fOr on the other hand on the other hand making your startup - isn't you (ideally). You are giving the arrangement. The issue is out there in the commercial center. For instance, individuals used to utilize accounting sheets to monitor great many clients, contacts, messages, and orders. Or, flagging down a taxi, riding in a taxi, paying for a taxi, and managing a terrible taxi driver is an awful encounter. Or, there are no lodgings in SFO during DreamForce and I utilize my summer home for precisely fourteen days every year and the remainder of the time it sits empty.

Those are all issue portrayals that don't have anything to do with Salesforce, Uber, or Airbnb. Those organizations tackle those issues with their items and administrations. The issue is the aggravation in a market space. Your answer is how you settle it. You should know - and obviously well-spoken - that distinction to your audience.

How big is the problem?

The issue you are tackling is your justification for being. It's your "why", and you ought to, please, weave an anecdote about how you came to know about, experience, and come to an answer for this issue. But you should also work to demonstrate the relative size of the problem. That's known as the "All out Addressable Market" (TAM).

All in all, how large an issue is this thing you're tackling?

That's a tough piece of information to know, and even tougher to slip into an elevator pitch. But it needs to be done. To start with, you really want to know the size of your market before you set off to assemble a business around it. Is it even large to the point of supporting a way of life business or a development startup? How would you know? That is the kind of data that works out easily from having lived, or encountered, the issue first hand.

Second, you really want to sort out a method for placing that number or set of numbers into your pitch. Here are a few models from pitches we've heard at Pitch Practice.

- "Like clockwork a bicycle iS taken in the U.S., and the normal expense of a bicycle is $400."
- "66% of twenty to thirty year olds have understudy loan obligation, and the normal obligation is $35,000."
- "60% of recent college grads are relinquishing their positions since they are not getting the administration improvement that they want."

Each of these - in one sentence or perhaps 3 seconds - gives a strong gander at the size of the market. Presently, assuming you're conversing with a financial backer, that financial backer could conceivably have a premium in that market, yet you'll arrive at that point much speedier when you show that you know the issue and the size of the market. One of the most terrible things you can do is convey a convincing pitch, and afterward not have the option to uphold it with genuine world data.

The all out addressable market (TAM) has a place in each pitch. In the event that conceivable, utilize genuine numbers that you've found in your exploration, instead of "I immovably accept" or "I feel that", since those expressions amount to nothing. Truth be told, utilizing such expressions will rapidly show to financial backers that you have no thought what you're referring to and that you haven't done any homework.

If you don't have the foggiest idea about the size of your addressable market, learn it first, before you pitch.

LESSON 8: The issue is the aggravation in a market space. Your answer is how you address it. You should know the difference.

LESSON 9: You have rivalry. Absolutely never say "we have no contest" anyplace in your pitch, or elsewhere besides. Your greatest rival is the norm, and getting individuals to significantly alter the manner in which they do things is unquestionably hard. On the off chance that you truly, really have no rivalry, you have found something far greater than you know, or there is no market for different contenders to enter.

Chapter 8 - Your Solution to the Problem

"You cannot be sure you really understand any part of any business problem unless you go and see for yourself firsthand. It is unacceptable to take anything for granted or to rely on the reports of others." - Eric Ries

Now that you've tracked down a major, awful issue in a huge market, and you can explain that issue so every head in the room gestures as your crowd "gets it", now is the right time to put words to your solution.

You find out about the issue you're addressing through client revelation, before you at any point assemble anything that scents like an item or administration, by requesting hundreds from individuals in the designated market (generally the space in which you have at minimum some area skill) and figuring out what their day to day aggravation is. Here is an incredible model from Atlanta's startup community.

- MailChimp – Creating and sending an email newsletter is horribly complicated and confusing, and the email service provider software UIs are awful.

Do you know what the arrangement is? You can most likely sort out it from the issue articulation, in light of the fact that MailChimp was begun from the acknowledgment of a terrible issue in an enormous market space. But their idea for a business was not what came first. The issue started things out. MailChimp was made to tackle the issue. The arrangement turned into the business.

After going to such torments to verbalize the issue you're tackling, how would you express your solution?

Don't Give Away The Store In Your Pitch

"You can encourage someone to go in a certain direction, but that person must ultimately decide for himself to water, however you can't make him drink," correct? Not a chance. A lie from the pit of hell.

That's right, you've been told a lie for a long, long time. I'll make sense of right away. For the present, consider your brief presentation. You have a limit of 30 seconds, accepting you stand out of your crowd. What would you be able to say in that time? Better inquiry: what would it be advisable for you say?

Before you answer that involving the time tested develop as the beginning stage for your pitch, think about this: what is the objective of the short presentation? To get the deal? No. To get a venture? No. The brief presentation has one objective and only one goal:

***To get the next meeting*.**

With that arrangement, what would it be advisable for you to say in your short presentation to achieve your particular objective? Here's a clue: *not everything*. You just have 30 seconds and one objective, and you presently realize that you should zero in on the issue. That ought to limit the focal point of your words very well, down to barely to the point of getting your crowd intrigued. At a new meeting of Pitch Practice, private supporter Charlie Paparelli made an exceptionally intriguing comment:

> ***"A good test of an elevator pitch is if it results in a meaningful discussion afterward."***

Brilliant! At the end of the day, your short presentation ought to be the flash, not the flamethrower, howitzer, or B52. Your pitch ought to get your crowd talking, get them intrigued, spark their interest for additional. Your brief presentation ought to get you to the following meeting.

Now, about that parched pony. In the event that you put salt in the pony's oats, he will drink when you get him to the water. Your contribute is the salt the oats of your crowd. Make them eager for more.

Are you "Uber for this" or "Match.com for that"?

It's difficult to make Yourself clear in a short brief presentation. You need to establish an extraordinary first connection, and you need to ensure your crowd "gets it". Yet, imagine a scenario in which you have a truly complicated offering or your market space isn't all around well known?

To help move past that obstacle, it might assist with thinking about a similarity (or three) that empowers your audience members to effortlessly comprehend what it is that you're doing. No relationship is awesome, yet commonly utilizing the right similarity can rapidly make yourself clear, particularly to your interest group. Here are some straightforward examples.

- Blockbuster video through the mail (Netflix)
- Email for sending somebody cash (PayPal)
- Lightweight MS Office in a program (Google Apps)

Those could help the perspective of thinking of a similarity that depicts your business thought. From late meetings of Pitch Practice, here are a portion of the similarities that have been utilized effectively.

- LinkedIn for proficient soccer players (Arenalinq)
- Uber for valet stopping (Luxe)
- A coding training camp for advertising innovation (DGM

Camp) Your business is like something, so assuming you're experiencing difficulty making sense of what you do, attempt to observe a decent, well known relationship that will assist anybody with getting your business. Only one out of every odd business has a pleasant relationship and few out of every odd pitch requires a similarity. And one should be careful when applying analogies, especially when you think you might use "Uber for X". That one has been utilized every which way in this new sharing economy.

Remember the KISS Principle

If you've obviously expressed the issue to the right crowd, then, at that point, portraying your answer can and ought to be extremely basic. Simply get out whatever your answer is:

- Software
- A portable app
- A website
- A device
- A service
- A community
- Software as a Service

Think back a couple of pages to the Calendly model: plan gatherings without the volatile messages. The exceptionally next question will be, “Alright, how would you do that?” Next gathering, please.

Whatever your answer is, simply express out loud whatever it is, however avoid depicting HOW it attempts to tackle the issue. Keep in mind, salt in oats. Zero in on the issue. Say the arrangement. Get the following meeting.

LESSON 10: If there’s a straightforward similarity you can utilize (e.g., “match.com for systems administration”), use it. Once in a while that makes it understood or genuine for your crowd. In any case, be cautious utilizing “Uber for___________________________________.” That can blow up on you in a hurry.

Chapter 9 - The Customer

"Get out of the building" - Steve Blank

Point number six in the Pitch Practice strategy for fostering your pitch is “who is the client?” We put this snippet of data in the brief presentation since, just subsequent to articulating the issue that you are addressing, realizing your client is the following most significant snippet of data that you can pass on to your audience.

After we’ve recognized an issue some place in a commercial center, the following thing we do is escape the structure, converse with however many possible clients as we can, and approve the issue. The Lean Startup calls this interaction client revelation. It’s not selling, since you don’t have an item to sell yet.

Customer disclosure is in a real sense finding who the client is and what they need and how they approach procuring items and administrations. The client is the element that is encountering the issue that you have recognized, approved, and tackled (or are currently settling). That substance will pay you cash for your item or administration at some point.

“Everyone” is not a customer

Just as significant as being incredibly explicit about the issue you’re addressing is as a rule strangely explicit about who your client is, particularly from the beginning in the existence of your business. It likely could be that the whole world could be your ideal interest group, yet when you're a 1 or 2 or 3 man startup, you can't market to, offer to, or support the entire world. Even Facebook started with a very specific user in mind: college students at Harvard. But let's not get confused here. There are clients and there are clients. Clients pay you cash. Clients don't. Facebook has 2+ billion clients, however we don't pay them cash. Facebook's sponsors pay them money.

Eventually, somebody needs to pay your startup cash, or you will not make due. Extremely, barely any new businesses can be like Instagram (2 years of age, 10 workers, zero income, offered to Facebook for $1 Billion), and no one in their right

brain would suggest that as a strategy.

So, in your pitch, it ought to be obvious to your crowd who your client is and the way in which you bring in cash, regardless of whether it's just about as straightforward as "it's a SaaS item for inside team leads." That tells us precisely who the client is and precisely the way in which the fanciful startup will bring in cash (subscriptions).

Who are you beholden to?

This example comes up a ton at Pitch Practice. The resulting conversation ordinarily works its direction back to the Facebook model I referenced before. Facebook has north of 2 billion clients, however they have huge number of clients (promoters) who pay them cash. Who is Facebook obligated to? Their customers.

When Facebook changes something in its UI or application or calculation, that is no doubt to help their advertisers.

Make sure that you can distinguish who your unmistakable, ideal, early client fragment is and that your crowd is evident that you have a deep understanding of your customer.

LESSON 11: Make sure you can recognize who your client section is and that you have a deep understanding of them.

LESSON 12: Traction rules. Assuming you have 10 or 20 or 100 elements utilizing (or paying for) your administration, you should share that reality. Assuming you have 10 clients, you're that a lot nearer to item showcase fit.

Chapter 10 - The Ask

"Be so good they can't ignore you." Steve Martin

The last piece of the Pitch Practice design of an extraordinary pitch is "the ask", and it's presumably the second most troublesome piece to get right. Most frequently, the issue articulation is the hardest, yet when you get that right, it doesn't change a lot of except if you make a turn. The "ask", be that as it may, could change each and every time you say your pitch on the grounds that your crowd and your requirements could change each time.

Gary Vaynerchuk refers to it as "hit, *hit, punch... right snare" or "give, give, give, give, ask.*" We need to give worth to our crowd before we acquire the option to request anything. That makes the ask in your pitch even harder and even more important. On the off chance that you don't offer some benefit to your crowd, your "inquire" will fall on hard of hearing ears.

In each pitch, you need to request All in allmething, on the grounds that sooner or later, as a business person, you must request cash, either from a client or a financial backer or both. So, you really should become accustomed to it, practice it, become familiar with it, since it's not going away.

With that as a primary concern, how do you have at least some idea what to request? Here are some ideas.

- Ask for something you have some control over, if conceivable. Assuming you're in a lift with Sig Moseley, and you get the chance to express out loud whatever you do, would you say you will give him your card, or would you say you will ask him for his? You ask him for his card and obviously request that his consent call and set up the following gathering (the unrivaled objective of the lift pitch).
- If you're fund-raising, that is your "inquire". Own it, however be specific:
    - Say precisely how much cash you are raising, and
    - Say the exact thing you will do with that money.
    - These two focuses, in blend, exhibit to financial backers that you've done your math.
- It is critical to Know your crowd. At Pitch Practice, the

objective is to improve, which requires criticism on your pitch. That is a simple method for working on requesting something explicit: “I would truly like your criticism on my pitch.” See how simple that is?

- If you need the crowd to follow through with something, like download your application or follow you on Twitter, make it truly simple for them to make it happen. It’s now that you realize if your Twitter handle or application name or site is not difficult to understand.
- If you're at an investor event, like Venture Atlanta, and the ask in your pitch is something like "Come by our booth", make it very specific, like "Please come to our booth number 1234 right in front of the Coffee Station".
- Remember that the crowd, but enormous or little, has allowed you to talk. Asking your crowd for something, in the wake of giving them esteem, makes it about them and not about you. Recall who the superstar is. Answer: it’s not you. It’s your audience.

Adjust to your crowd, especially with your inquire. At the point when you pitch, you are quite often requesting something, regardless of whether it’s “Decision in favor of us to win!”, so you ought to (a) know your crowd before you pitch and (b) become exceptionally familiar with requesting anything it is you need from your crowd. It very well may be references, guidance, input, a vote, or on the other hand assuming you’re pitching financial backers, money!

Ask for something you have some control over, whenever the situation allows, yet consistently, consistently request something.

Every Startup Needs Something...Different

You shouldn’t have to fund-raise, or you probably won’t be prepared to fund-raise yet. Yet, that doesn’t mean you want nothing. What do you need?

- A cofounder
- Beta users
- A mentor
- An advisor
- A developer
- Customers
- Referrals
- A particular hire

Whatever you want, request it explicitly. In the event that you don't request it, you won't ever get it. What's more, when you truly do request it, be incredibly, explicit about that one thing that you're asking for.

In any pitch, basically the same as an advertising point of arrival having an extremely clear Call To Action (CTA), you need to have an exceptionally clear inquire. That implies request a certain something and one thing as it were. What do you need the most right now? Ask for it until you get it, then move on to what you need most then, and ask for it.

LESSON 13: Adjust your pitch to your crowd, especially with your inquire. Know your crowd before you pitch and become exceptionally familiar with requesting anything it is you need from your audience.

LESSON 14: When you say you're fund-raising, say an accurate sum and say it with zeal: "We're raising $500k." You are never "hoping to raise" cash. You are "raising" X dollars to achieve Y and Z, period. Own it.

Chapter 11 - Tell Us A Story

"The audience does not need to tune themselves to you. You need to tune your message to them. Skilled presenting requires you to understand their hearts and minds and create a message to resonate with what's already there." - Nancy Duarte

We can draw something other than one place of motivation from Simon Sinek's TED Talk and book, "Begin with Why". Probably the simplest technique for attracting your crowd to a comprehension of you, your business, or your startup is to recount the narrative of why you are doing what you are doing.

- How did you find the issue you're solving?
- How did you approve the issue in the marketplace?
- How did you concoct the solution?
- How did you come to the heart of the matter of choosing, "Indeed, I can begin a business to do this"?

- How did you get your first customer?

Each of these is a story. To your crowd, the best of which ought to be individuals in the market who are experiencing the issue you're addressing and individuals who have a monetary stake on the off chance that the issue can be settled, your story implies the world!

An extraordinary model is New Story Charity, and, indeed, the name fits too. Brett Hagler had gone on a mission excursion to Haiti after the 2010 tremor had obliterated the homes of thousands of individuals there. He saw direct what it resembled to live in a cardboard tent with wrongdoing, sickness, and starvation all over. That is the means by which he learned of and approved the center issue. He additionally found out about the issue with the then current "arrangement" to the genuine problem.

The Red Cross, a worldwide charity with billions of dollars in assets, had fabricated 6 homes there in 5 years, predominantly because of the unadulterated administration of the association. Brett and his fellow benefactors realized there had to be a superior method for raising assets and construct practical homes for families in Haiti and somewhere else. So they established New Story, and assembled 100 homes in 100 days.

Telling a story improves everything. There's an explanation that fiction is so famous. Individuals love a story, and while you're pitching a business, your story is about how the business became. The narrative of the issue not entirely settled to tackle will strike a chord with your target group. Had Brett Hagler just caught wind of this issue and not experienced it direct, his story wouldn't be so compelling.

(And, no, the fabulous utilization of the name "New Story" isn't lost on me.)

Nancy Duarte's TED talk is a huge resource and guide about how to recount your story. Narrating isn't irregular. It's not made up. There's a deductively based design for how to really recount a convincing story, when you have one to tell. What is the account of how your startup became? Tell that story!

Little Red Riding Hood

Do you know how old Little Red Riding Hood was? How old was her grandma? What was in that bushel? How enormous was the wolf? How far did the wolf follow the young lady? This multitude of raw numbers don't make any difference, since you recollect the story, not the real factors and details. Exactly the same thing applies to your pitch. Your crowd will recall a convincing story, yet they will neglect even the most astonishing realities or statistics.

That doesn't mean you don't recount those realities that help your pitch, however you mesh them into a story that everybody will remember.

LESSON 15: Telling a story improves everything. There's an explanation that fiction is so famous. Individuals love a story, and while you're pitching a business, your story is about how the business became. The tale of the issue not entirely set in stone to tackle will strike a chord with your expected audience.

Chapter 12 - Now Grow Your Elevator Pitch

"One of the ways you convey the operational excellence is in the quality of the plan." - Marc Andreessen

In a short presentation, you are it: your words, non-verbal communication, timing, ask… everything. But if you're doing a pitch with a slide deck, that changes the dynamics of your presentation quite a bit. Here's one method for drawing closer doing such a show, paying little heed to how long or short that show is.

Your slides are the cake. You are the icing. This is a pleasant approach to saying that your slides ought to have practically zero text by any stretch of the imagination ever, except if it's totally essential. We have the interwebz, so you can track down an image to delineate anything, or you can utilize Fiverr and pay somebody a couple of bucks to make a picture that represents your point. Then you tell the story behind that picture, much like Instagram: image first, then tell the story.

Are there exemptions for this "no text by any means ever" rule? Certainly, yet that ought to be your beginning stage. Whenever you are introducing, ask yourself one question:

Do you want the audience to have their eyes on you or on your slides?

There are times when you need the crowd to truly see something on your slide. At those times, it is fitting to be quiet and permit your crowd a second to absorb anything it is you need them to see. But at all other times, your slides are the cake, and you are the icing. They ought to be checking out at you the whole time. As far as you might be concerned, that implies you should order their attention.

For your slides, it implies that they should make a point rapidly, and afterward empower the crowd to pull together back on you for the story or clarification behind that specific slide. The following are 4 focuses to go by while making your slide deck for a presentation.

- An image tells 1,000 words
- People read at various speeds
- Text is exhausting, pictures rock
- Our cerebrums interaction pictures quicker than text

With these as a top priority, similarly as you can utilize the Pitch Practice structure as the exceptionally beginning stage for your short presentation, utilize the "no message by any means ever" rule as the beginning stage for your pitch deck. Begin with 0, and work from that point. Assuming you in all actuality do need to add message, ensure it's brief and huge.

Engage Your Audience During A Presentation

Giving a drawing in show is difficult work. Certain individuals are normal speakers, yet a large portion of us need practice, input, and direction to further develop our introducing abilities. I used to show the Digital Marketing class at General Assembly's Atlanta area, I actually run the week by week Pitch Practice meetup of business visionaries each Friday in Atlanta, and I lead a few other little gatherings in different other capacities.

Over the years, I've introduced on many times to a wide range of individuals - financial backers, clients, workers, loads up, understudies - and I've discovered that there are five strategies that, utilized reliably, will assist you with keeping any crowd engaged.

1. Ask questions - Also known as the Socratic strategy, you instruct by posing inquiries to the crowd. Then you have instant material when you use the audience's answers in your talk. All the more

critically, posing inquiries offers you the capacity to sparkle consideration on various individuals in the room, which completely draws in those people. Individuals love to recount their own story, so ask them open-finished inquiries about their experiences.

2. Tell a story - Tell stories that your crowd can connect with. This implies that you need to know your crowd. Realizing your crowd is essential for your schoolwork for any show, and it can help you with what inquiries to pose, yet in addition with everything sorts of stories you can say to that the crowd will totally connect with. I as of late driven a class on contributing to a blog for your image, and presented myself by let the crowd know that I started publishing content to a blog 10 years prior when my better half and I ventured out across the globe to adopt our two kids. The reaction to that story was amazing.
3. Use Humor - This doesn't actually imply, "make wisecracks." Unless you're an expert, making quips can be dangerous. Rather, use humor in recounting your accounts. Carry humor to your own mix-ups, and your crowd will immediately connect with your experiences.
4. Move around - If you are not behind a platform, move around the floor, so you can look at changed individuals without flinching. Eye to eye connection is the main human association we can have with someone else. At the point when you look at somebody without flinching, you are undeniably more associated with them than if you don't look. To make this statement, take a stab at having a discussion with somebody you know, and never look at them without flinching. They will plainly imagine that you are concealing something from them. A similar idea applies to conveying an incredible presentation.
5. Memorize Your Presentation - Memorizing what you will say requires practice. While you're giving any show, you're selling yourself, so you ought to rehearse a considerable amount before any show, huge or little. I prescribe rehearsing to the place of retention. Whenever you stagger on words, your crowd sees, regardless of whether you're great at act of spontaneity. At the point when you convey your words with certainty, no notes, and without taking a gander at your slides (assuming you're utilizing any), the crowd insight is that you know the material and invested in some opportunity to get ready. You took more time for them.

When you plan well for a show, you'll be more sure as you move around, look at people without flinching, ask them inquiries, and recount to silly stories that the crowd can connect with. These five straightforward strategies can have a gigantic effect in your capacity to introduce yourself or your organization to any audience.

LESSON 16: You possess energy for 5 slides in a 3-minute pitch. Overall, the vast majority talk for 2-3 minutes for each slide in a show. Having more slides doesn't make a superior pitch.

LESSON 17: Video is denied, except if it's ridiculously cracking great. I've just seen video in a pitch work precisely one time. Be cautious with video.

LESSON 18: Your slides are the cake. You are the icing. You can track down an image to represent anything, or utilize Fiverr and pay somebody a couple of bucks to make a picture that delineates your point. Like Instagram: image first, then tell the story.

LESSON 19: If you're contributing a challenge, you should, in all seriousness pay the
$100 to get a professional to plan your slides with as couple of words as could be expected and wonderful visuals. There's simply not a viable alternative for an incredible design.

Chapter 13 - The Final Lesson

"Be yourself; everyone else is already taken." - Oscar Wilde

Remember, great correspondence is reliable and dreary. There are 6 things that you should remember for your 30-second pitch:

1. Your name
2. Your organization name
3. The problem
4. Your customer
5. Your solution
6. Your ask

It takes practice. In any case, you can remember every one of the watchwords and expressions you need to, and let them out in a real lift or extended financial backer gathering, yet that will not get you to a higher level. But here's the advice that will.

Are you prepared for it? Since it's difficult. Here goes.

Be yourself.

Not what you needed to hear, right? You must act naturally. While you're pitching a startup with no functioning item, no paying clients, and no income, think about the thing the financial backers are purchasing? You.

So, convey every one of the extravagant remembered canned pitches you need, yet don't feel that one impeccably conveyed 3-minute/4 slide show will land you a sweet seed round. You must be so comfortable and alright with your item, your space, your financial aspects, your rivals, your interaction, and your future that it's important for what your identity is and how you speak.

The objective of the brief presentation is to get to the following gathering, and you won't
have a content. You'll need to depend on your capacity to be yourself.

LESSON 20: When the startup is only the thought, YOU are 100 percent of the startup, and any individual who trusts in the startup is having faith in you. Act naturally.

www.ingramcontent.com/pod-product-compliance
Lightning Source LLC
LaVergne TN
LVHW041259150826
845673LV00008B/2651

* 9 7 9 8 8 0 0 4 1 3 8 3 0 *